Dwayne's Guitar Lessons Presents:

Strumming To Success

A Beginner's Guide To Acoustic Guitar

By
Guitar Teacher
Dwayne Jenkins

Copyright © 2025 Dwayne Jenkins.
All Rights Reserved.
Published by Tritone Publishing

Introduction

Welcome to the wonderful world of playing acoustic guitar! A world where anything is possible. No matter if you are picking up the guitar for the first time, or revisiting it after a long break, this guide will help you to find the joy of playing acoustic guitar.

The acoustic guitar is a versatile and widely beloved instrument. Perfect for relaxing, strumming along to your favorite songs, or creating your own music. No matter what purpose you choose, the acoustic guitar can help get you there.

Acoustic guitars are an excellent choice for beginners due to their portability and simplicity. Unlike electric guitars, acoustic guitars do not require cables or amplifiers. This makes them easy to pick up and play anywhere you choose.

They are perfect for playing by yourself, or for accompanying a singer, or even playing in a group. For these reasons, the acoustic guitar is very popular in many styles of music. Including, Folk, Pop, Jazz, Rock, and Country.

Being that this is the case, you will be able to play the acoustic guitar for years. Even if your musical tastes change over time. As I previously stated, the versatility of the instrument will allow you to fit into just about any style of music.

In this comprehensive course, you will learn the inner workings of playing the acoustic guitar. The type that is best to choose when starting. How to hold the guitar. As well as the chords that are best to start with.

This helpful training guide has been engineered to give you a clear and straightforward step-by-step method of study. Allowing you to progress at a rapid rate. That is if you follow the method exactly as it has been laid out.

Strumming To Success is loaded with diagrams, notation, and pictures for easy learning. These will allow you to build a foundation that all your future studies will be able to stand on. Which will give you a skill that can last for a lifetime.

Dive into the world of acoustic guitar with this comprehensive guide designed for beginners. Learn essential techniques that will allow you to strum your way to success, and have fun in the process.

Dwayne Jenkins

Table of Contents

Introduction 1

Chapter 1 Introduction To Acoustic Guitar 1

Lesson 1: The acoustic guitar 1
Lesson 2: Types of acoustic guitars 4
Lesson 3: Choosing the right guitar for you 7
Lesson 4: How to hold and handle the guitar 9
Lesson 5: Chapter 1 Quiz 13
Chapter 1 Summary 15

Chapter 2 Getting Started With Basics 17

Lesson 6: Understanding guitar anatomy 17
Lesson 7: Getting your guitar in tune 19
Lesson 8: First steps in holding a pick 21
Lesson 9: Reasons for using a pick to start 23
Lesson 10: Chapter 2 Quiz 25
Chapter 2 Summary 27

Chapter 3 Essential Chords & Transitions 29

Lesson 11: Introduction to open chords 29
Lesson 12: Practicing chord changes 31
Lesson 13: Building muscle memory 33
Lesson 14: Basic chord progressions 37
Lesson 15: Chapter 3 Quiz 40
Chapter 3 Summary 41

Chapter 4 Strumming Techniques 43

Lesson 16: Basic strumming patterns 43
Lesson 17: Counting beats and timing 45
Lesson 18: Developing consistent rhythm 47
Lesson 19: How to use a capo 50
Lesson 20: Chapter 4 Quiz 52
Chapter 4 Summary 54

Chapter 5: Introduction To Fingerpicking 55

Lesson 21: Basic fingerpicking patterns 55
Lesson 22: Coordinating your fingers 57
Lesson 23: Using fingers and a pick together 59
Lesson 24: Tips for effective practice 61
Lesson 25: Chapter 5 Quiz 63
Chapter 5 Summary 64

Chapter 6 Reading Guitar Notation 65

Lesson 26: Chord charts & more chords 65
Lesson 27: Reading guitar tabs 68
Lesson 28: Regular sheet music 70
Lesson 29: Benefits of reading guitar notation 72
Lesson 30: Chapter 6 Quiz 74
Chapter 6 Summary 75

Chapter 7 Introduction To Basic Theory 77

Lesson 31: Understanding scales and keys 77
Lesson 32: The root of chords in music 80
Lesson 33: How chords and scales relate 81
Lesson 34: Build confidence through understanding 82
Lesson 35: Chapter 7 Quiz 83
Chapter 7 Summary 84

Chapter 8: Overcoming Challenges 85

Lesson 36: Common beginner mistakes 85
Lesson 37: Tips for staying motivated 87
Lesson 38: Setting musical goals 88
Lesson 39: Develop a practice routine 89
Lesson 40: Chapter 8 Quiz 90
Chapter 8 Summary 91

Strumming To Success Conclusion 93

Chapter 1 Introduction To Acoustic Guitar

Lesson 1: The acoustic guitar

The acoustic guitar's history can be traced back thousands of years to ancient civilizations that used stringed instruments with sound boxes. These primitive designs laid the foundation for the evolution of the guitar to what we know today.

Europe is where the guitar first began to take shape. First characterized by a basic body with four strings, and eventually being introduced with frets. This addition influenced the guitar's playing style and versatility.

Over time, significant changes were brought to the design of the guitar. The instrument had evolved into a guitar with 5 strings. This allowed the strings to be tuned in unison or octaves, for more complex compositions.

As the guitar continued to evolve, the 5-string guitar eventually became a 6-string guitar. Which resembles the modern acoustic guitars we see today. This additional string allowed for a wider range of composition and musical expression.

In the 19th century, the acoustic guitar had a significant turning point. With advances in manufacturing, it improved the guitar's overall quality. This allowed for better accessibility and established it as a solo instrument.

Throughout the next century, the acoustic guitar started to cement itself in popular music. Musicians embraced the instrument for its portability and rich sound, which allowed them to craft songs that had appeal the world over.

All this was accomplished because of details given to the instrument's construction. Luthiers like Orville Gibson and C.F. Martin developed enhancements that projected the sound and increased the tonal quality.

Today, the acoustic guitar remains one of the most loved and widely played instruments around the world. Its enduring appeal lies in its versatility, ease of use, and the emotional range that can be easily produced.

No matter if you're using it for a single performance, ensemble groups, or singing around a campfire, the acoustic guitar continues to inspire and connect people around the world through its timeless sound.

The acoustic guitar remains one of the most versatile and popular instruments in the musical family. Its ability to be learned quickly and carried around easily is what makes it so popular.

Whether in a small coffee house or a large concert hall, the acoustic guitar's natural sound is known to captivate audiences. An instrument that is highly preferred by both beginners and professionals.

With modern technology, acoustic guitars are better than ever because they now have built-in features. Such as tuners, and electronic pickups. These allow them to be amplified to keep up with a band without losing their natural tone.

Thanks also to the creation of the digital world, guitar players can learn quickly. Online resources, that provide a wealth of information. From books, videos, online courses, and private instruction.

In addition, this allows for a guitar player at any skill level to learn in the comfort of their home. So with all this being said, get yourself an acoustic guitar and start enjoying the fun of playing it today.

Lesson 2: Types of acoustic guitars

Acoustic guitars come in a variety of shapes, sizes, and colors. Which caters to the unique needs and preferences of modern musicians. From dreadnoughts to parlors, each one has characteristics that influence both their sound and playability.

The different body shapes and sizes are designed to produce certain sound qualities, making certain guitars more suitable for particular music styles. This variety allows players to select a guitar that complements their style and musical taste.

Dreadnought:

This is one of the most popular and recognizable types of acoustic guitars. Known for its large body and powerful sound, it offers a balanced tone with a strong bass response. This makes it an excellent choice for strumming and playing in bands.

Concert:

Concert and grand concert guitars are slightly smaller than dreadnoughts, offering a more comfortable fit for some players. They produce a bright, clear tone that is well-suited for fingerpicking and light strumming.

Auditorium:

Auditorium guitars strike a balance between the dreadnought and the concert. They offer a versatile sound, suitable for both fingerpicking and strumming. Great for solo performances and recording sessions due to their well-rounded tonal qualities.

Parlor:

Parlor guitars are smaller-bodied instruments that deliver a warm and intimate sound. Guitars are perfect for blues, folk, and slide guitar playing, offering a focused tone with clear articulation.

Understanding these different types of acoustic guitars will help you make an informed decision when selecting the right instrument for your musical journey. Each type offers distinct advantages and can significantly influence your playing experience and sound.

Lesson 3: Choosing the right guitar for you

Selecting the right acoustic guitar is an important step in your musical journey, as it greatly influences your playing experience and sound. With so many options available, it can be overwhelming to find the perfect match.

However, by considering a few key factors, you can narrow down your choices and make an informed decision. Here are five crucial aspects to consider when choosing your acoustic guitar.

Size and comfort:

The first consideration when choosing an acoustic guitar is its size and how comfortable it feels when you play it. Guitars come in various shapes and sizes, from the small and portable parlor guitars to the large and resonant jumbo guitars.

Try different sizes to see which one fits comfortably in your hands and against your body.

Sound & tone

Each type of acoustic guitar offers distinct sound qualities, so it's important to find one that matches your preferences. For instance, dreadnought guitars are known for their powerful, balanced tone.

This makes them ideal for strumming and playing in groups. On the other hand, concert and grand concert guitars produce a bright, clear sound, well-suited for fingerpicking.

Budget & quality:

Acoustic guitars are available at a wide range of prices, from budget-friendly options to high-end models. Set a realistic budget before you start shopping and explore guitars within that range.

Consider the genre of music you enjoy and play most often, and choose a guitar that complements that style. Testing different guitars in person will give you a better sense of their tonal characteristics.

Lesson 4: How to hold and handle the guitar

Once you have found the guitar that is right for you, it's time to learn how to hold and handle it.

To properly hold and handle an acoustic guitar, sit up straight with the guitar resting on your right leg. The guitar body should rest comfortably against your chest, with the neck angling slightly upward.

Position your fretting hand on the neck, ensuring your thumb is placed at the back for support and your fingers are curved to press down on the strings. Your strumming or picking hand should hover over the sound hole or behind the bridge.

Allowing for smooth movement. Maintain a relaxed but firm posture to help maintain control and prevent strain during extended practice sessions.

Fretboard Hand Position:

Position your fretting hand on the neck, ensuring your thumb is placed over the top or in the back for support. Ensure your fingers can press down on the strings as this is essential for holding chord shapes.

Curve your fingers naturally so that they arch over the strings, enabling you to press down on them without muting other strings. Aim to use the tips of your fingers for pressing, which will help produce clear, crisp notes.

Keep your wrist slightly bent but relaxed, avoiding excessive tension that could lead to discomfort or strain. This posture will facilitate smoother transitions between chords and more precise finger placements, enhancing your overall playing technique.

Once you get your fretboard hand in the proper position, you want to work next on your picking hand. It is the ability to work both hands together that is necessary for proper acoustic guitar playing.

Strumming Hand Position:

Your strumming or picking hand should hover over the sound hole or just behind the bridge, allowing for smooth movement. Keep your posture relaxed but firm, as this will help maintain control and prevent strain during extended practice sessions.

 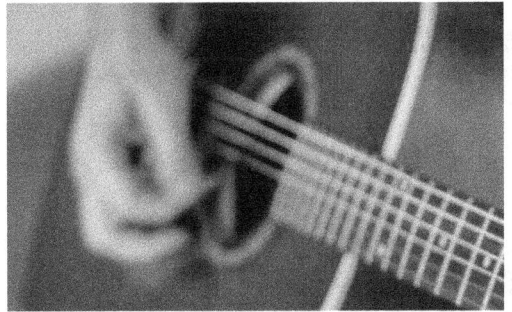

Your picking hand posture is crucial for achieving a smooth and effective playing technique on the acoustic guitar. Whether you are strumming or picking individual strings.

Ensure that your hand is not too tense, as this can hinder your ability to play with precision and control. Keep your fingers slightly curved and flexible,

Let's take a look at some more examples of these postures.

Here we can see the instrument is held comfortably, and the strumming hand is relaxed and positioned over the sound hole.

In this example, the strumming hand is a bit further back by the bridge, which can also be used to strum certain chords.

These postures will help you maintain a consistent rhythm and dynamic range, enhancing your overall playing experience.

Lesson 5: Chapter 1 Quiz

In this lesson, I have taught you some basic fundamental principles of playing guitar. Now comes the part to see how well you learned the lessons.

If you're not too sure about an answer, no need to worry. They are all in this chapter. So just go back and find it.

Q: In the medieval age, the guitar begins to take shape where?
A: _____

Q: In early 20th century, what luthiers enhanced the sound?
A: _____

Q: Modern guitars have built-in features such as?
A: _____

Q: What guitar is known for its large body and powerful sound?
A: _____

Q: What unique qualities does the auditorium guitar offer?
A: _____

Q: What is the first consideration in choosing a guitar?
A: _____

Q: What is ideal for strumming and playing in groups?
A: _____

Q: Testing guitars in person will give you a better sense of?
A: _____

Q: To properly hold and handle an acoustic guitar you?
A: _____

Q: How do you best position your fretting hand?
A: _____

Q: The position of your picking or strumming hand should be?
A: _____

Q: Your picking hand posture is crucial for achieving what?
A; _____

Knowing the answers to these questions will set up a strong foundation for your musical education. It will also make sure that your acoustic guitar playing is off to a proficient start.

Chapter 1 Summary

In this first chapter, we explore the rich history and evolution of the acoustic guitar. Tracing its origins from ancient stringed instruments to the modern six-string we know today. This perspective helps appreciate the instrument.

We then look at different types of acoustic guitars available, highlighting the unique features and tonal qualities of each. From the widely known dreadnought to the more compact parlor.

Another focus in this chapter is the process of selecting the right guitar for a learner's individual needs. It discusses key factors to consider when choosing an acoustic guitar. Such as size, sound, quality, and budget.

The chapter concludes with essential guidance on how to properly hold and handle a guitar. It offers tips for posture, positioning, and technique to ensure beginners can play comfortably and effectively.

This foundational advice serves as a critical stepping stone for beginners as they progress through subsequent chapters and develop their skills further.

16

Chapter 2 Getting Started With Basics

Lesson 6: Understanding guitar anatomy

The guitar is made up of basically two key components. Each contributes to its overall sound and playability. The body of the guitar and the neck.

Within these two components, you have a sound hole, bridge, pickguard, tuning pegs, frets, fret markers, strings, nut, fretboard, and a headstock.

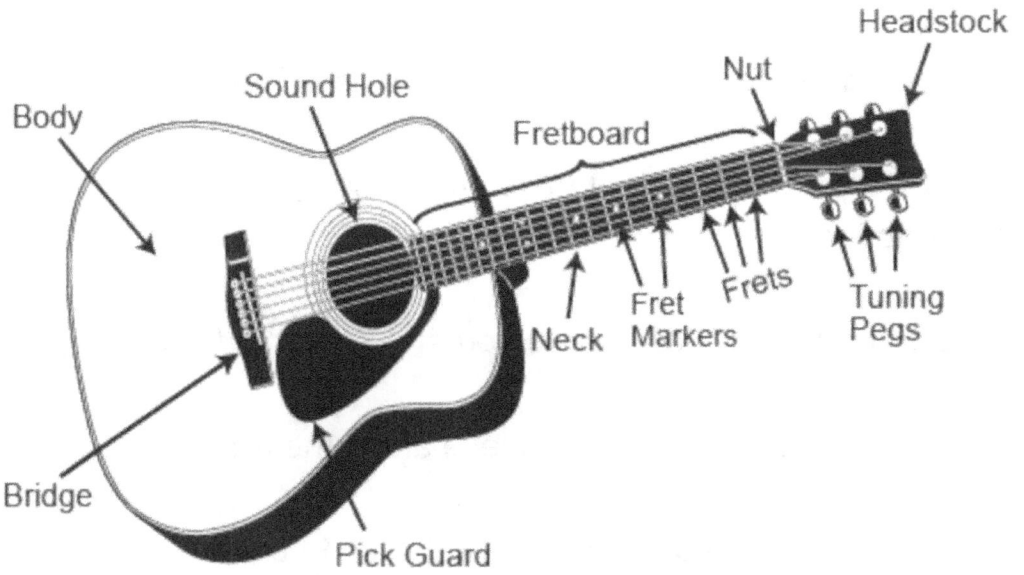

Body: What you hold on to when strumming or picking the strings.

Bridge: Holds the ends of the strings in place on the body.

Soundhole: Amplifies the string's vibration through the body.

Pickguard: Protects the body from getting scratched by the pick.

Neck: Serves as a base for the fretboard where you press down on the strings.

Fretboard: Where you form guitar chords up & down the neck.

Frets: Control the pitch of the strings when pressed down on the fretboard.

Fret markers: Indicate where you are along the fretboard.

Nut: This holds the strings in place along the fretboard.

Strings: These create vibration and pitch to create music.

Tuning pegs: Allow you to tune strings to pitch

Headstock: Holds the tuning pegs in place.

Lesson 7: Getting your guitar in tune

Having your guitar in tune is one of the most important lessons you will need to master when it comes to playing guitar. So make sure to get this lesson learned well.

To ensure your guitar is in tune, begin by using an electronic tuner or tuning app.

I recommend something like this.

Clip-on guitar tuner:

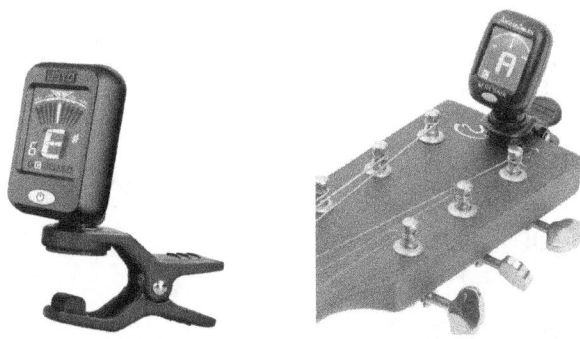

An electronic tuner that easily clips onto the headstock of the guitar. It is easy to use and has a big bright display that is easy to read.

20

Guitar tuning app:

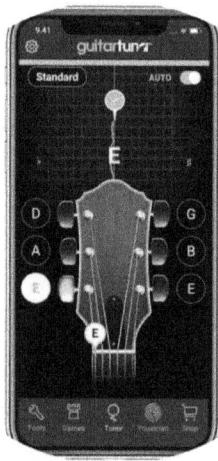

This is a great option because you can download it to your phone and have it with you at all times.

When tuning the guitar you will tune it to standard tuning. This is where each string will be tuned to a certain pitch.

This tuning is **E-A-D-G-B-E** from the lowest (thickest) string to the highest (thinnest) string. It will ensure that your guitar chords (if properly played) will sound like music to the ear.

Regular tuning checks will help maintain your guitar's sound quality and playability.

Lesson 8: First steps in holding a pick

Once you get your guitar in tune, you then want to get a guitar pick and learn how to hold it. This is one of the fundamental skills you'll need to develop.

The pick, also known as a plectrum is a small tool that is used to strum or pluck the strings. Mastering its use can greatly enhance your sound and playing technique. These come in many different materials and colors.

Guitar pick:

 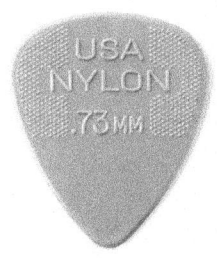 

I recommend you try out a few different ones and see what type works best for you. Playing the guitar is very personal and the pick you use will highly affect what you can get out of it.

Once you find the pick that feels right in your hand, you want to learn how to hold it. This is done between the thumb and the first finger.

Holding the guitar pick:

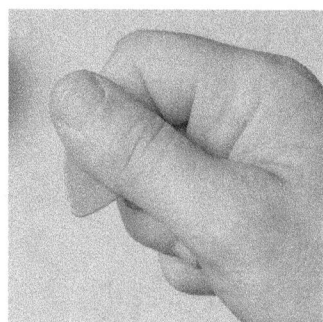

As you can see from the picture above, the pick is placed between the thumb and first finger with the pointy part sticking out. This is what will be used to strum across the strings.

Here is another example of the pick in the playing position. Held between the thumb and first finger slightly angled. This is perfect for strumming across the strings.

Practice daily with a pick, which will help you develop an articulate percussive attack upon the strings. This will produce more precise playing and a brighter sound.

Lesson 9: Reasons for using a pick to start

Starting with a pick offers several distinct advantages that can be particularly beneficial for beginners. Here are some compelling reasons to consider using a pick as you embark on your guitar-playing journey.

Improved sound clarity:

Using a pick often results in a clearer and more articulate sound compared to finger strumming. Picks also provide constant contact with the strings, allowing each note to ring out distinctively.

Easier to learn strumming patterns:

For those just starting, strumming can be one of the more challenging aspects of playing the guitar. A pick simplifies the process by providing a uniform tool to execute strumming patterns.

Enhanced finger dexterity:

Using a pick can help develop the finger dexterity needed for more advanced guitar techniques. Holding and maneuvering a pick requires coordination between the thumb and finger, which lays the groundwork for finger independence.

Versatility across musical styles:

A pick is a versatile tool that allows players to explore a wide range of musical styles. From rock and pop to folk and country, many genres utilize picking techniques to achieve their characteristic sound.

Develops consistent playing habits:

Finally, playing with a pick can help develop consistent playing habits that are crucial for long-term success. Learning to use a pick involves developing proper grip and strumming techniques, which can prevent bad habits from forming.

As beginners gain confidence with a pick, they build a solid foundation that supports their growth as musicians. Thus enabling them to tackle more complex pieces with ease.

All these benefits make using a pick an excellent choice for beginners eager to develop their skills and explore the world of acoustic guitar music.

Lesson 10: Chapter 2 Quiz

Presented is a simple test for chapter two. As before, it is to make sure you know the material well.

Remember, if you don't know an answer, go back and look through the lesson. All answers will be found there.

Q: What two key components is the guitar made up of?
A: _____

Q: What are the 12 parts of the acoustic guitar?
A: _____

Q: What is the purpose of the guitar fretboard?
A: _____

Q: What lesson in this chapter is most important to master?
A: _____

Q: What two types of guitar tuners are recommended?
A: _____

Q: What is beneficial about a guitar tuning app?
A: _____

Q: What is a guitar pick?
A: _____

Q: What is the best way to hold the guitar pick?
A: _____

Q: What is another name for a guitar pick?
A: _____

Q: What do picks provide constant contact with?
A: _____

Q: Using a pick can help develop what?
A: _____

Q: What are consistent playing habits crucial for?
A: _____

The lessons in this chapter help to forge the basis for playing the acoustic guitar and lay the foundation for more advanced techniques.

Chapter 2 Summary

Chapter 2 focuses on laying the groundwork for successful guitar-playing by starting with the basics. Guitar anatomy, tuning the guitar, using a pick, and reasons why it is beneficial.

First, you are guided through the parts of the guitar anatomy. Helping them understand the function and importance of each component.

Second, you learn about two types of guitar tuners to use and what pitch to tune your guitar to. By mastering this lesson, you can ensure your guitar will always be ready for optimal performance and sound quality.

Third, you learn about what a guitar pick is. A simple tool that is used when. Strumming the guitar strings. You learn how to hold the pick between your thumb and first finger, as well as place it in the proper position for maximum efficiency.

Fourth, you learn about reasons why it is beneficial to start out using a pick. Learning to hold and handle a pick correctly contributes to producing clean articulate sounds. While laying the foundation for more advanced techniques.

Chapter 3 Essential Chords & Transitions

Lesson 11: Introduction to open chords

Open chords serve as an excellent starting point for beginners. These chord types are typically played with two or three fingers using a combination of open strings and fretted notes.

Open E minor chord

This chord requires only two fingers. Both the middle and third fingers on the 5th and 4th strings of the second fret.

Open D chord

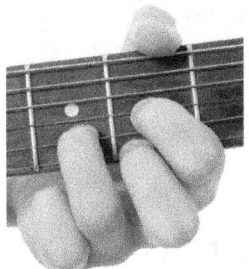

Place your index finger on 3rd string second fret, middle finger 1st string second fret, and third finger on 2nd string third fret.

Open G chord:

Place your middle finger on the 6th string third fret, your index finger on the 5th string second fret, and your third and fourth fingers on the two bottom strings of the third fret.

Open C chord:

Place your third finger on the 5th string third fret, your middle finger on the 4th string second fret, and your index finger on the 2nd string first fret.

These four chords will set the foundation for your guitar chord vocabulary. Practice forming them daily. As you progress in your studies, you will learn other chord shapes in the chapter on reading music notation.

Lesson 12: Practicing chord changes

Transitioning smoothly between chords is a crucial skill for any aspiring guitarist. As a beginner, you'll want to start with the chord presented in the previous chapter. E minor, D, G, and C, which are commonly used in a variety of songs.

Begin by placing your fingers in the correct positions for each chord and practice holding the position for a bit. This will help to build muscle memory. Then practice switching between them slowly and deliberately.

It's important to focus on the correct finger placement for each chord and minimize any unnecessary finger movement. As you practice, try to keep a steady rhythm and gradually increase your speed as you get more comfortable with the transitions.

As you work with transitioning between chords, start by switching between just two at a time. G to C, or G to E minor. As you get more comfortable with this, work on incorporating the D chord. Many songs are made up of only three chords.

Try to practice daily. Even for a very short period, regular practice is key to developing proficiency and building confidence in your playing.

To further enhance your chord transition skills, experiment with different strumming patterns (which you will learn in an upcoming lesson) while changing chords. This will help you to learn the fundamental principles of playing songs.

Additionally, practice transitioning between chords while humming or singing along to a song. As you get better at changing chords, you'll begin to hear songs that you already know. And this is where the fun comes in.

As you do that, think about what chord is coming ahead before you change to it. Take time holding the chord before you switch to the next one. Work at counting to four before you change to the next chord. This will help with timing.

Focus on keeping your fingers close to the fretboard when changing chords as this will minimize finger movement. In addition to that be sure to take breaks from time to time. This will help with controlling fatigue and stamina.

By dedicating time and effort daily to these exercises, you will soon find yourself changing between chords easily and effectively. But remember, it will take time to accomplish. That is why daily practice is necessary.

Now let's learn about building muscle memory.

Lesson 13: Building muscle memory

Building muscle memory is a crucial aspect of becoming proficient in playing the acoustic guitar. It involves training your muscles to perform specific movements automatically, allowing you to play smoothly without thinking about it.

This process is essential for mastering chords, strumming patterns, and fingerpicking techniques. As it enables you to focus on musical expression and creativity rather than the mechanics of playing.

Building muscle memory takes time and dedication. But with consistent practice daily, you can greatly enhance your guitar-playing abilities.

Consistent practice and repetition:

The foundation of building muscle memory lies in consistent practice and repetition. Begin with simple exercises that focus on basic chord transitions. By repeatedly practicing these movements, your fingers will start to memorize their positions and the pressure required to produce clear sounds.

Just 15 to 20 minutes daily can reap huge rewards over time.

Breaking down complex techniques:

When learning more complex techniques it is always best to break them down into smaller, manageable parts. Focus on mastering each segment individually before combining them into a complete piece.

This approach allows your muscles to become accustomed to each specific movement, making it easier to integrate them into a cohesive unit.

As you practice each segment, pay attention to the nuances of finger placement and movement, ensuring precision and efficiency. Over time, these smaller components will seamlessly come together through muscle memory.

Incorporating visualization:

Visualization is a powerful tool that can complement physical practice in building muscle memory. Spend a few minutes each day mentally rehearsing the guitar techniques you are currently working on.

Visualize your fingers moving across the fretboard, changing chords, and going through strumming patterns. This mental practice reinforces neural pathways. Helping to solidify muscle memory even when you are away from your guitar.

By combining visualization with committed physical practice daily, you can enhance your learning process and reinforce the skills that you are learning. Which builds a solid connection between the mind and body.

Being proficient as a guitar player is not only physical but mental as well. You must not only develop your physical skills but also your mental faculties.

Eye-hand coordination is where this takes place. The more this skill set is developed, the more confident you will become in your abilities. That is why consistent practice daily is so important at the very beginning of your musical journey.

Patience and perseverance:

Like they say "Rome wasn't built in a day" and so will this be with you and your guitar. It won't come in a day, or even a week, But stick with it, and it will come.

Building muscle memory is not an overnight process. It requires patience and perseverance. It's common to encounter frustration, especially when progress seems slow or mistakes persist.

However, maintaining a positive mindset and understanding that muscle memory develops gradually is key to overcoming these challenges. Especially in the very beginning.

Celebrate small victories along the way, such as smoother chord transitions, or a much clearer strumming pattern. Remember, every practice session contributes to your overall growth.

By engaging in all these things mentioned in this lesson daily as you progress in your studies, you will enhance your speed of progress. Both physically and mentally as you train your fingers to move automatically.

Always be aware of your progress. Celebrate where you are getting better, and double down on where you need improvement. By doing this daily you will stay motivated to push through frustration and minor setbacks.

Remember, embrace the process, and enjoy the journey.

Lesson 14: Basic chord progressions

Now that we have all the basics out of the way, we can look at basic chord progressions. This is where the rubber meets the road,

Step one is to form the individual chords.

Step two is to switch between chords.

Step three is to go through chord progressions.

This is what songs are made out of. Forming chords, and strumming them in a certain sequence.

Understanding and practicing basic chord progressions is essential for any aspiring guitar player. Chord progressions form the backbone of most popular songs and provide a framework for musical expression.

Here are some common chord progressions that utilize the chords that you have previously learned and have (hopefully by now) been working on forming and switching between.

These will help to solidify all that you have learned up to this point in the training.

The one-four-five progression:

Out of all the progressions, this is by far the most popular. It involves the 1st, 4th, and 5th notes of a scale. In the key of G major, these chords would be G, C, and D. G is the 1, C is the 4th, and D is the 5th note of the G major scale.

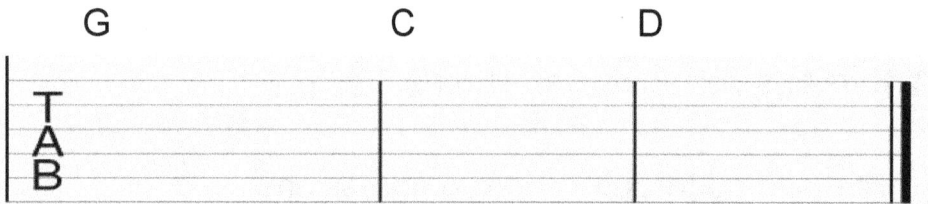

This is a 3-bar measure using the 1-4-5 progression.

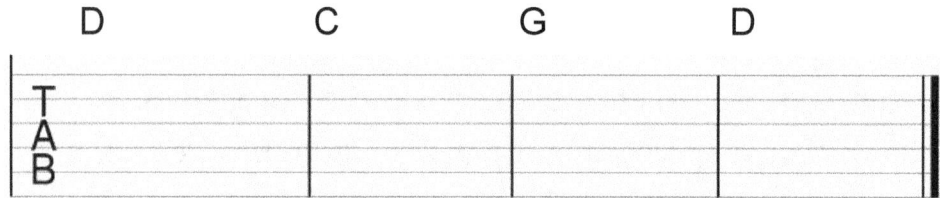

A 4-bar measure using the same chords in a different order.

Another common chord progression is similar but uses all 4 chords learned so far. The 1-6-4-5. In the key of G major, these would be the same as above, but we'll add the E minor chord to the progression.

The one-six-four-five progression:

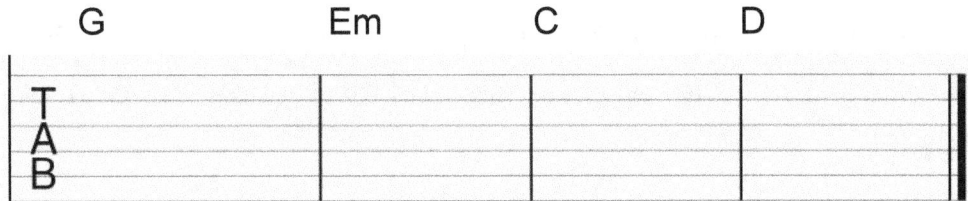

In this example, we have added the E minor chord to create a different progression.

Since we decide to use the sixth of the key (which is a minor chord) we use E minor because E is the sixth note in the key of G major.

As we progress in the training, we will learn more about this in further detail. But for now, just work with the chords that you've learned so far.

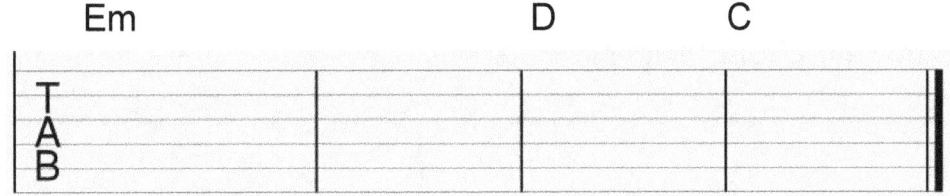

This progression uses 3 chords, but the first chord plays for two bars, and the last 2 play for one bar each.

Work with these and listen to how they sound.

Lesson 15:   Chapter 3 Quiz

Here you learn about the fundamentals of playing chords. This is the starting point for all guitarists and the foundation for many songs.

Q: What type of chords serve as an excellent starting point?
A: _____

Q: What are the four chords learned in this chapter?
A: _____

Q: How important is finger placement when forming chords?
A: _____

Q: Lesson 13 is based on what important aspect of playing?
A: _____

Q: What are chord progressions?
A: _____

Q: Why are chord progressions important to know?
A: _____

With this chapter, you are now beginning to make music. So study and practice daily.

Chapter 3 Summary

In chapter three we have learned about the fundamentals of building a strong foundation in chord playing. This is crucial for any aspiring guitarist.

It introduces open chords which are fundamental to many songs and provides a starting point for beginners. These chords are the building blocks of countless musical pieces, making them an essential part of the guitarist's repertoire.

By mastering open chords you can begin playing recognizable songs and begin to build confidence in your abilities.

There is also an emphasis on the importance of practicing chord changes, a skill that often challenges beginners. Transitioning smoothly between chords is vital for retaining the rhythm of a song.

To facilitate this, the chapter offers practical exercises aimed at improving finger placement and coordination. These exercises are designed to help develop muscle memory, which is crucial for executing chord changes.

Building muscle memory is key as it enables guitarists to perform chord changes with speed and accuracy.

The chapter provides tips and techniques to reinforce muscle memory such as repetitive daily practice. By focusing on these exercises, you can achieve a more fluid playing style.

In addition to individual chord practice, you are presented with basic chord progressions. These are simple yet effective learning tools designed to introduce you to the inner workings of popular songs.

Utilizing the chords learned earlier gives insight into how you might put them together in a cohesive sequence, which fosters a deeper understanding of song structure.

This helps to develop a sense of musicality and creativity. The exploration of chord progressions not only enhances technical skills but also visualization.

By focusing on open chords, smooth transitions, building muscle memory, visualization, and chord progressions, you will build a solid foundation on your musical journey.

Chapter 4 Strumming Techniques

Lesson 16: Basic strumming patterns

Strumming is an essential technique to master for any acoustic guitarist. This will allow you to utilize your pick to create music.

Understanding and mastering basic strumming patterns provides a solid foundation that allows you to bring life and music to your chords. Let's explore some fundamental strumming patterns that every beginner should know.

Downstroke strum pattern:

The simplest strumming pattern begins with the downstroke, where you strum across the strings downward with your pick. For practice purposes, strum down 4 times per chord.

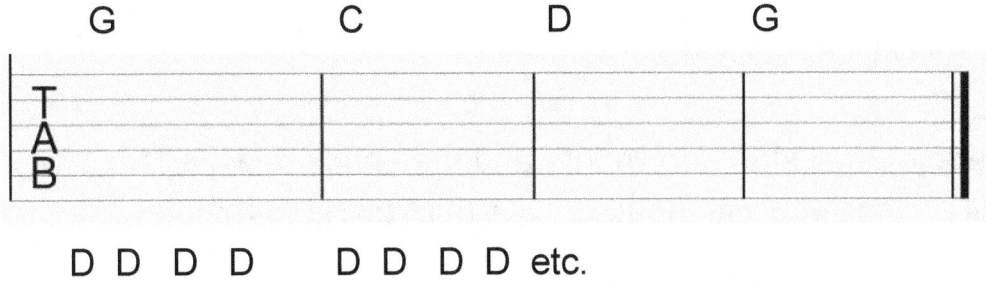

D D D D   D D D D etc.

Once you have that accomplished, you want to add the upstroke to your strumming.

Down and upstroke strum pattern:

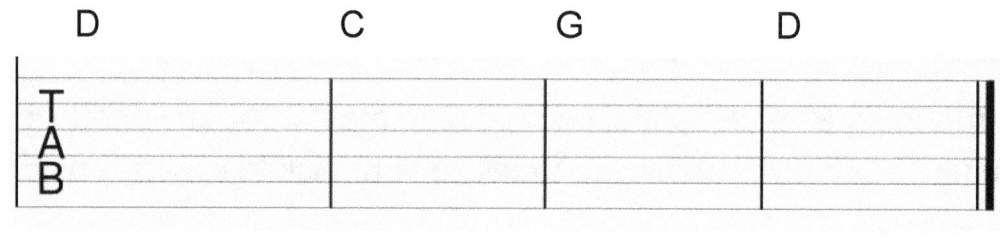

D U D U D U D U etc.

Here you will strum down and then back up. Repeat this process to give you a different rhythm pattern.

Down up down strum pattern:

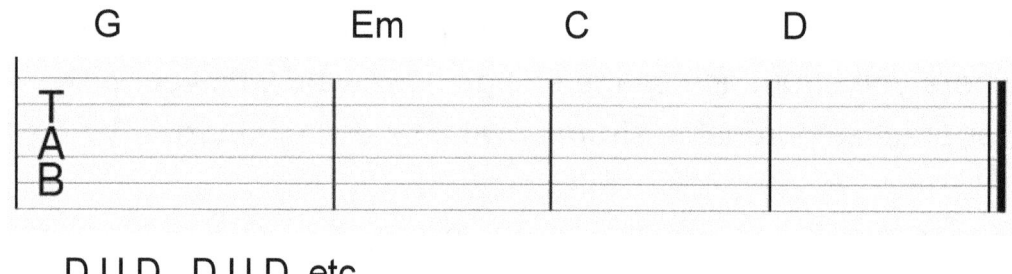

D U D D U D etc.

Here you will strum down, up, and then back down again. This will provide you with another type of strumming rhythm.

All these are found in many common songs, so make sure to practice them daily. They will build the motor skills necessary to play more complex strumming patterns later on.

Lesson 17: Counting beats and timing

Understanding beats and timing is fundamental to mastering rhythm on the acoustic guitar. In musical terms, a beat is the basic unit of time, the pulse of the music that you tap your foot to.

Example of 4 measures:

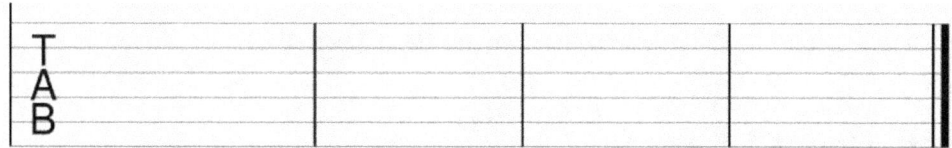

We saw this in the previous lessons when we talked about chord progressions and strumming patterns. One of these sections would be considered 1 measure.

Quarter notes: four per measure

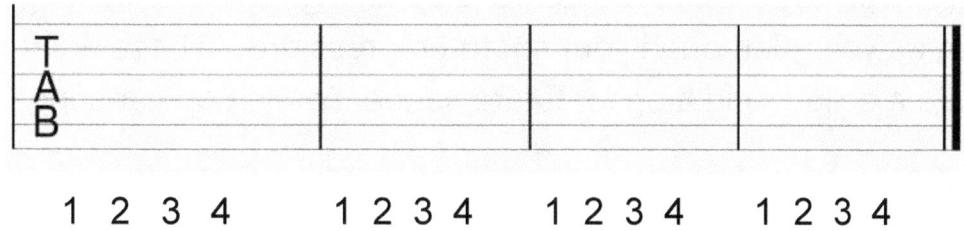

The next one is the eighth note. Two quarter notes tied together.

Eighth notes: count 1 & 2 & 3 & 4

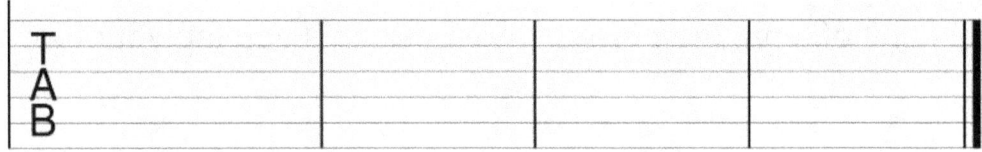

1 & 2 & 3 & 4 & etc.

Next comes the triplet. Three notes tied together.

Triplet: Count 1 & uh

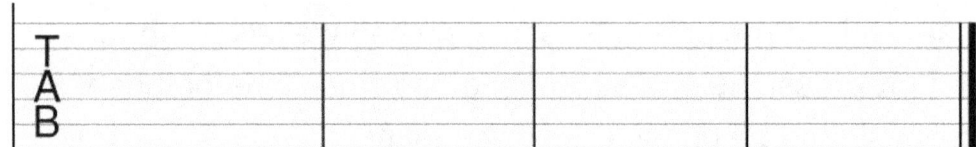

1 & uh 2 & uh 3 & uh etc.

Practice these three counts to develop timing. Work on mixing them as you go through your chord progressions. These will create a solid foundation for future sequences in popular songs.

Lesson 18: Developing consistent rhythm

Developing a consistent rhythm should be the goal for every guitarist. Especially in performance. No matter if you are a soloist or play with an ensemble.

Mastering rhythm involves understanding how to maintain a steady pulse while playing, which ensures that your music flows smoothly and aligns with other musicians if you are playing in a group.

One effective way to build this skill is through the use of a metronome. Practicing with a metronome helps you to internalize the beat, ensuring that you stay on time, even while transitioning through chord changes.

Types of metronomes:

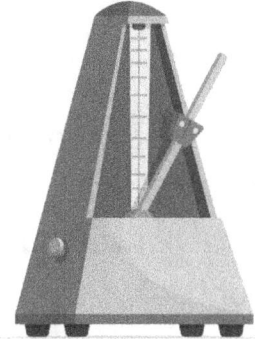 

A metronome is a great tool for the specific purpose of developing consistent rhythm. Using a metronome and counting out loud while playing can reinforce a strong sense of timing.

By counting you establish a direct connection between the rhythmic pattern and your physical playing, and you enhance your ability to navigate through variations of different rhythms.

Practice exercises that emphasize syncopated or off-beat rhythms can be highly beneficial with the use of a metronome as it will help you with counting these odd-timing rhythms.

Playing with recordings:

Another way to enjoy the development of timing and rhythm is by listening and playing along to recordings of your favorite songs. This method allows you to feel the natural flow of music as you mimic the timing and dynamics of the song.

Use this method to pay attention to how rhythm sections in bands maintain the groove and how guitar parts fit within that framework.

By actively listening and playing along, you not only improve your timing but also develop a deeper understanding of how rhythm contributes to the overall feel of a piece of music.

Finally, engage in rhythmic exercises that focus on developing both your internal sense of timing and your physical execution. This can be done through exploring different musical styles.

Practice tapping your foot as well as clapping the rhythmic pattern of the song to solidify the beat, the timing, or the strumming pattern of the song.

Recording yourself is another great way to analyze your progress when it comes to developing rhythmic timing. As you listen back to the recording, you can check your timing and see what needs improving.

By dedicating time daily to these exercises, you build a solid rhythmic foundation, enhancing your overall musicianship. Enabling you to express yourself more confidently through your playing.

Lesson 19: How to use a capo

What is a capo?

A capo is a small device that allows you to play your open chords further up the neck. It acts as a moveable nut. Which determines the pitch of the instrument.

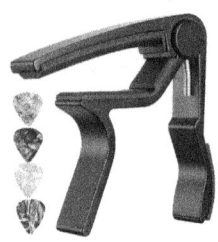  

The role of the capo

As you can see from the pictures above, the capo is a device that clamps on the fretboard. It allows you to play chords further up the neck. This changes the key of the music, without having to change your chord voicings.

There are many different types of capos, and the pictures above show a few examples. These devices are very common among guitar players who play both acoustic and electric.

When you press the strings down on the fretboard, you change the pitch of the strings. This changes the key of the music. The capo allows you to do this quite easily. Allowing you to play your open chords further up the neck in different keys.

You can also use the capo with barre chords. It is highly recommended you learn these types of chords as well. As they allow you to move quickly up and down the fretboard when not using a capo.

The difference between using a capo and using barre chords is that the capo can only be put in one position at a time within a song, whereas where barre chords can be freely moved up and down the fretboard during a song.

I recommend getting a capo and working with it in different positions along the fretboard. You will see very quickly how handy it can be as an addition to your guitar playing.

Lesson 20: Chapter 4 Quiz

In Chapter 4 you have learned about bringing the chords you learned in the previous chapter to life. This is done through strumming and fingerpicking. Two very common ways to play the acoustic guitar.

Knowing how to approach the guitar in these two ways, will help you to establish rhythm, which is essential to playing any instrument.

Q: What is strumming?
A: _____

Q: What are strumming patterns?
A: _____

Q: Why are strumming patterns important to know?
A: _____

Q: What is a beat in music?
A: _____

Q: What is the time value of a quarter note?
A: _____

Q: What is the time value of an eighth note?
A: _____

Q: What is the time value of a triplet?
A: _____

Q: What does maintaining a steady pulse master?
A: _____

Q: What tool helps to internalize the beat?
A: _____

Q: What do you directly establish by counting?
A: _____

Q: What does playing with your favorite songs accomplish?
A: _____

Q: What is a capo?
A: _____

Q: What are some benefits of using a capo?
A: _____

This chapter is essential to creating and understanding rhythm. The better this skill is developed, the better your guitar playing.

Chapter 4 Summary

In chapter four we have learned some very important techniques. These are what will be used to bring your chords to life and help you establish a rhythm.

First, we take a look at basic strumming patterns, These are what bring your guitar chords to life and make them sound like music.

We then look at counting beats and timing. Crucial elements in creating rhythm and staying on time while going through your chord progressions.

Learning to develop a consistent rhythm comes next. Creating rhythm is one thing, but keeping it consistent over time is something else. You must work on this skill set daily to master it. Better rhythm equals better guitar playing.

Lastly, the chapter goes over the use of a capo. A very common accessory to guitar playing. It can help you to easily play your open chords further up the fretboard. I recommend you get one, and use it.

Chapter 5 Introduction To Fingerpicking

Lesson 21: Basic fingerpicking patterns

In addition to strumming the chords to create music, you can also pick the strings with your fingers. This technique is called fingerpicking or fingerstyle.

As you can see from the pictures above, you will use your fingers to play the strings instead of a pick. In this approach, you play the chords individually instead of all together like strumming.

In this chapter, we will look at a few simple picking patterns to help you develop this approach. As you progress with this style, you'll see how it will give you a softer sound.

Once you get it down, you can add it to your strumming to create versatility in your music.

Fingerstyle picking patterns:

```
T|-----------1--|-----------1--|-----------1--||
A|--------0-----|--------0-----|--------0-----||
 |-----2--------|-----2--------|-----2--------||
B|--3-----------|--3-----------|--3-----------||
```

In this example, you are fingerpicking the C chord. You form the chord as usual and then pluck the strings with your thumb, index, middle, and ring fingers.

Here is a similar pattern that you can use with the D chord. Thumb on the open string and other three fingers on the other notes.

This one is similar, but it uses the E minor chord. Start with your thumb on the low string and pick the rest with your fingers.

These are just examples to get you started with this style. Work on them with all the chords and chord progressions that you've learned in previous lessons.

Lesson 22: Coordinating your fingers

Fingerpicking on an acoustic guitar requires precise coordination of your fingers to produce clean and melodious tunes. This can only be achieved through daily consistent practice.

Establish a solid foundation in finger position.

As you can see from the picture above, the positioning of your fingers is vitally important.

Begin by familiarizing yourself with the basic finger positioning: Your thumb should be responsible for the bass strings E A & D. The index, middle, and ring finger, should be positioned over the G B & high E strings.

Master this for effective finger-picking.

Finger coordinating exercises:

Exercise #1

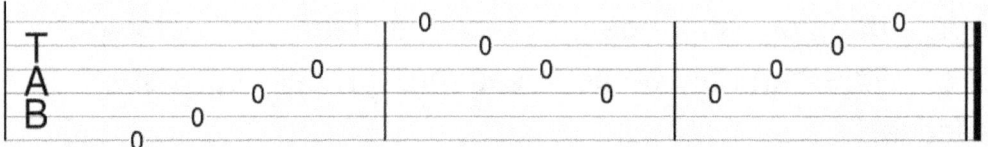

Exercise #2

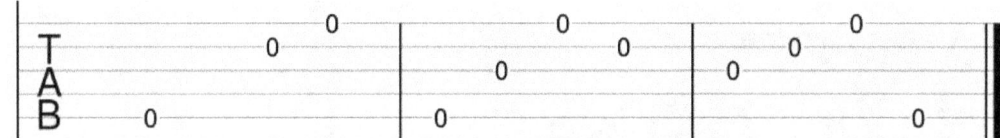

Exercise #3

Focusing on finger independence is highly important for training your fingers to move the way you want them to. This can be achieved through dedicated exercises.

Start with simple patterns like these, and be aware of this last one that uses two fingers at once. These will help you to build finger independence when practicing daily.

Lesson 23: Using fingers and a pick together

Using both fingers and a pick in your guitar playing allows for more diversity and expression. This technique, often referred to as "hybrid picking", combines the precision and attack of a pick, with the softer side of using your fingers.

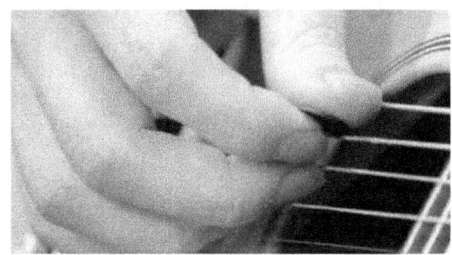 

This allows for both strumming and finger-picking styles to be combined. Allowing for a more versatile playing style.

By learning to integrate this technique into your playing, you can expand your musical repertoire and develop a unique sound that highlights both rhythm and melody.

Getting comfortable with hybrid picking:

Practice alternating between using the pick and your fingers by going over chords and chord progressions you have learned in previous lessons. This will help you to develop the necessary dexterity and control of your fingers.

Techniques and patterns:

One effective way to practice hybrid picking is to use the fingerstyle picking patterns that you have already learned. Instead of using your thumb and three fingers, you hold the pick and add your pinky.

Start with basic patterns, such as alternating between the pick and your middle finger, then gradually incorporate your ring and pinky fingers.

Exercise # 1

Exercise #2

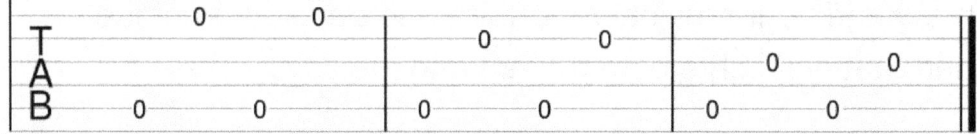

These exercises will build dexterity in your fingers and develop the proper execution in this style.

This technique will allow you to create more intricate and more expressive musical passages.

Lesson 24: Tips for effective practice

When practicing this style of playing (fingerstyle and hybrid picking) consistency and patience are key. Make sure to focus on maintaining a steady rhythm and even tone between your fingers.

Use a metronome to help keep your timing precise.

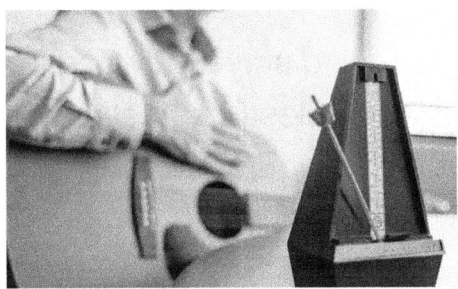

Be mindful of your hand positioning to avoid unnecessary tension, which can hinder your mobility and accuracy. When hybrid picking, experiment with different pick thicknesses and finger placements.

This will allow you to feel comfortable and produce the sound you desire. Remember, everyone plays differently, so you will need to practice daily to develop what works best for you.

Set clear concise goals:

One of the most important aspects of effective practice is setting clear achievable goals for each session. Before you begin, outline what you hope to accomplish. This will help you to structure your practice sessions for maximum efficiency.

Address specific challenges:

This will allow you to track your progress and stay motivated to overcome challenges. Setting achievable milestones helps you maintain a sense of accomplishment and encourages continuous improvement.

Practice consistently:

Another key element of effective practice is consistency. Rather than practice for long infrequent sessions, aim for shorter, more frequent practice times. Daily short practice can yield higher results than a few hours once a week.

Lastly, ensure that your practice environment is conducive to learning. A place where you can focus without distractions. Make sure your guitar is in good shape and all study material is readily available.

Lesson 25: Chapter 5 Quiz

In this chapter, you have learned the basics of fingerpicking. Another common style of playing acoustic guitar. This approach produces a softer gentler sound.

Q: How is the finger-picking style different than strumming?
A: _____

Q: The thumb is used for what strings in this style?
A: _____

Q: What strings do the index, middle, and third fingers play?
A: _____

Q: Why are picking patterns important to study?
A: _____

Q: Why is the fingering position so important in this style?
A: _____

Q: What is hybrid picking, and why is it useful in this style?
A: _____

Adding fingerstyle to strumming is a great way to enhance your musicianship and overall understanding of the acoustic guitar.

Chapter 5 Summary

Chapter 5 dives into the wonderful world of fingerpicking, opening new dimensions of acoustic guitar playing and introducing the fundamental techniques, focusing on the coordination of the finger's independence.

By going through basic finger-picking patterns you can create intricate and melodic soundscapes. This emphasizes the importance of developing precision and accuracy, as these enhance skill levels.

To get the best of the fingerstyle approach, you must learn to coordinate your fingers. This is done through daily practice of finger positioning exercises. Aligning your fingers to the proper strings will develop this style.

In addition to fingerstyle, you can also use the pick and fingers together. This technique allows for more diversity and expression in your playing. Practice alternating between using the pick and your fingers.

Also, to practice effectively, focus on setting clear achievable goals to help maintain direction and motivation. Maintain an organized workplace and a daily positive mindset to celebrate victories and overcome challenges.

Chapter 6 Reading Guitar Notation

Lesson 26: Chord charts & more chords

The first type of guitar notation that you will come across is chord charts. These are diagrams that will help you visualize chord shapes and finger positions. Like the ones you previously learned.

Chord chart:

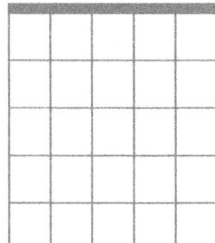

The vertical lines represent the 6 strings of the guitar, 6th to 1st from left to right. The horizontal lines indicate the first 5 frets on the fretboard.

The chord shapes will be indicated by dots on the guitar strings on certain frets. When looking at chord charts, the guitar is facing upward. The thicker horizontal line represents the nut that holds the strings in place.

Open E **Open D**

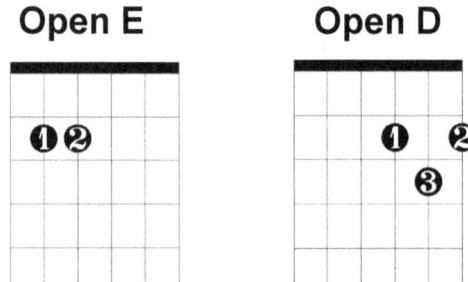

Here are the first two open chords you learned. E minor and D. The numbers on the dots indicate the fingers used to form the chords. Pay attention to what strings and what frets are being used for each one.

Open G **Open C**

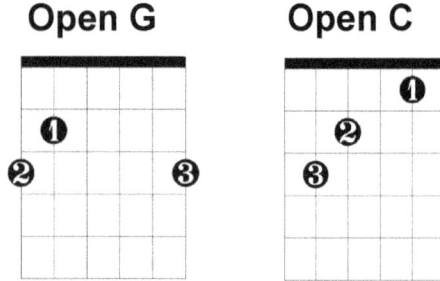

Above are the other two chords that you previously learned. The open G and open C chords. Once again, the diagrams show you the finger position, strings, and frets. Great for practicing your visualization skills.

When forming these types of chords, be sure to use the tips of your fingers. This will allow open strings to ring out and not get muted when strumming or fingerpicking them.

Now that we know how to read chord charts, we can look at other common chords used in many songs. This will help grow your chord vocabulary, and enhance your musical creativity.

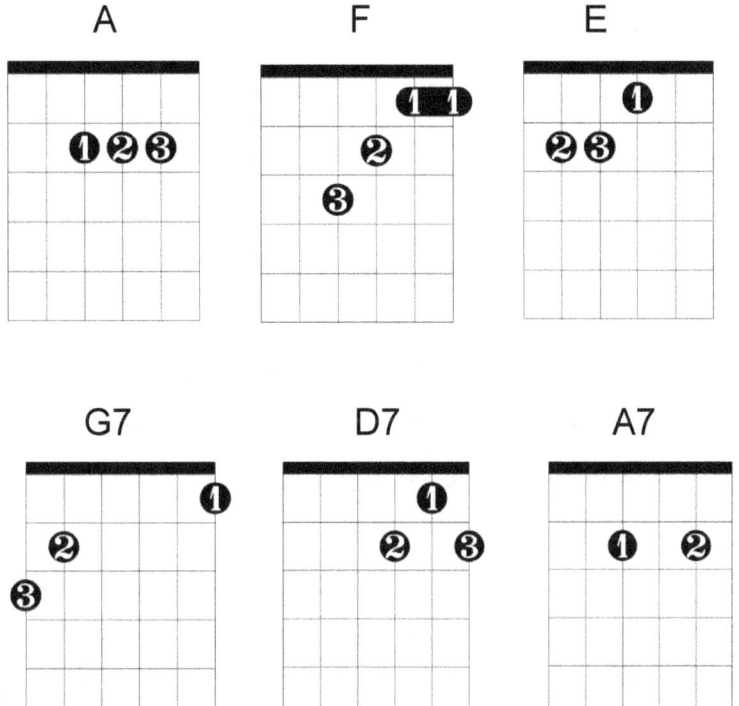

Use these chords to create chord progressions. Don't worry about some of the names, (G7, D7, etc) you'll learn more about that in later lessons. For now, just work with them and get familiar with how they sound.

Lesson 27: Reading guitar tabs

The next type of nation to learn is guitar tabs or tablature. A simplified form of sheet music designed specifically for guitar players. It allows you to learn songs quickly without having to learn traditional sheet music.

Guitar tab:

Tabs consist of 6 horizontal lines that represent the guitar strings. Starting from the low E string at the bottom to the high E string at the top. Upside down from your guitar fretboard.

Numbers are placed on the lines to indicate which frets to press on each string, guiding players on how to play chords, melodies, and guitar riffs.

Unlike standard notation, tabs don't convey rhythm or timing, so it's helpful to listen to the song to understand how the notes should be played.

The simplicity of guitar tabs makes them easy to understand and accessible for beginners who are just starting. Allowing for quick learning and application.

Chords in tab format:

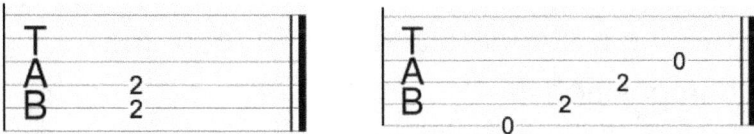

Here we have the E minor chord. If the notes are stacked above each other, this is for strumming, and if they are slanted at an angle, that is for finger-picking.

This is the D chord in the tab. Same thing as above. Stacked for strumming, and slanted for playing the notes individually.

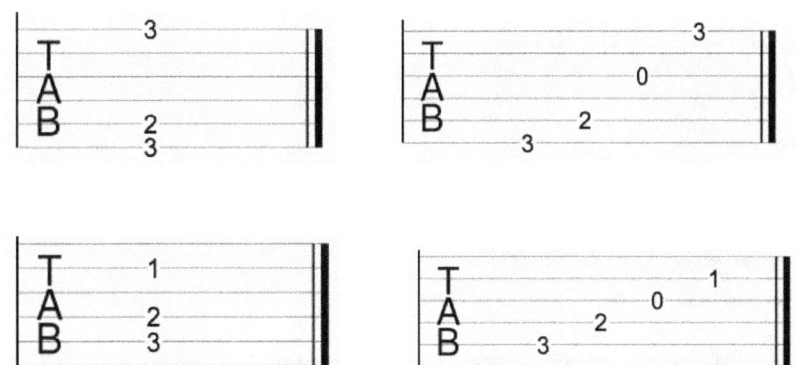

Here are the G and C chords. Remember, the low E string is on the bottom and the high E string is on top when reading tabs. Study these, they will come in very handy later.

Lesson 28: Regular sheet music

Regular sheet music (standard notation) is a universal language for musicians. Providing a standardized way to read and interpret musical compositions.

Unlike guitar tabs that primarily show finger placements on the guitar's frets, regular sheet music offers a more comprehensive representation of music by including musical notes, rhythms, dynamics, and articulations.

Although this is better in the long run, it can be a bit much for the beginner just starting. That is why guitar tabs have become the norm for reading sheet music as a guitarist. Keep it simple and get to having fun playing.

Sheet music basics: Staff lines

Sheet music is written on staff lines. Horizontal lines are like tabs, except there are only 5 lines, and here you use the spaces as well. As with tabs, you only use the lines, not the spaces.

Clefs & notes names: Treble clef.

Each line and space of the staff corresponds to a musical pitch, which is determined by the clef. There is a treble clef and a bass clef. For guitar, you use a treble clef because guitar is a higher-pitched instrument.

Along with the treble clef, the note names on the spaces of the treble clef spell out F A C E, and the note names on the lines are E G B D F. To help remember these, you could use an acronym like Every Good Boy Does Fine.

Chords in standard notation:

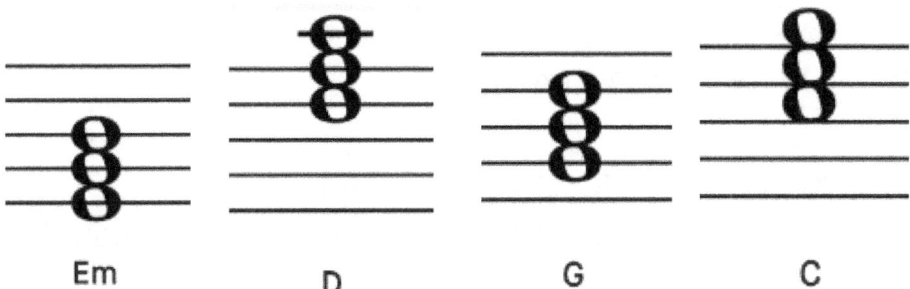

These are just the basics of standard notation, but as you can see, this is more difficult to understand than guitar tabs. It's why tabs are so popular when reading sheet music for guitar.

Lesson 29: Benefits of reading guitar notation

Understanding and being able to read guitar notation is an invaluable skill for any guitarist. No matter your skill level, you can always enhance your playing by learning to read sheet music. Here are some benefits.

Enhance musical understanding:

Reading guitar notation allows you to gain a deeper understanding of music theory. You'll learn how harmonies, melodies, and rhythms are constructed.

Improve sight reading skills:

By learning to read notation you improve your ability to sight-read music. This skill enables you to play new pieces more quickly and enhances your overall musicianship.

Access to a wider range of music:

Guitar notation opens up a vast library of music. Many compositions in many different styles are written in notation. Allowing you to explore pieces of music you might not normally be able to play.

Better communication with other musicians:

Understanding notation helps you to communicate more effectively with other musicians. It provides a universal language that everyone can easily speak.

Development of technical skills:

Reading and playing from notation challenges your technical skills. It requires precise timing, rhythm, and finger placement. Contributing to your overall growth as a guitarist.

Enhance memory and visualization skills:

Learning to read music notation can help improve your memory and visualization skills. It exercises your brain and improves eye-hand coordination. Along with focus and concentration.

Ability to learn complex pieces:

Notation provides detailed instructions on how to play complex pieces. These details allow you to tackle more challenging compositions with confidence.

By embracing musical notation, you not only enhance your musical horizons but also develop a well-rounded skill set that enriches your journey as a guitarist.

Lesson 30: Chapter 6 Quiz

In this chapter, you learn about guitar notation and the different types. This will give you insight into music construction.

Q: What is guitar notation?
A: _____

Q: What are chord charts?
A: _____

Q: What are chord charts?
A: _____

Q: What is standard notation?
A: _____

Q: What are staff lines in standard notation?
A: _____

Q: What do the spaces in standard notation spell out?
A: _____

Reading guitar notation is a skill; if you take the time to develop it, you will see enhanced musicianship over time.

Chapter 6 Summary

In this chapter, we have learned some basics about reading three different types of guitar notation. These are common that you will run into and it is highly recommended that you learn to read at least one, if not all.

The first type you will come across is called chord charts. These are box diagrams that quickly show you how and where to form a guitar chord along the fretboard.

In chapter 6 you learn how the chords previously learned are indicated in this format. E minor, D, G, and C are all presented. In addition to them, additional chords are presented to help increase your chord vocabulary.

The second type of guitar notation that is presented is guitar tabs. This is a shorthand way of writing music for fretted instruments. A visual guide that shows which strings to play and what frets to press down on.

Guitar tabs are a great way for beginners to learn songs quickly. They are more intuitive than traditional sheet music and are a great option for students who don't read traditional musical notation.

Also, remember that the horizontal lines represent your guitar strings, the biggest on the bottom and the thinnest on top, with each line having a number that indicates which fret to play.

Lastly, the chapter takes a basic look at standard notation. This is regular sheet music that to the untrained eye, can look a bit confusing, but to the trained eye, it makes sense.

With staff lines, clefs (treble for guitar), and symbols to represent the notes. In tabs, notes are indicated by numbers, in standard notation, they are indicated by symbols.

In standard notation, notes are written on the staff in alphabetical order from A to G and include the spaces between the lines as well. I recommend starting with chord charts and guitar tabs, as they are easier to learn from.

Guitar notation has a lot of benefits, and it would be wise to add reading it to your skill set. It will enhance your overall playing in ways that just playing by ear cannot.

Remember, these are the fundamental principles of reading guitar notation. And they will come in very handy when it comes to learning songs quickly.

If you learn to read sheet music of any kind, over time, it will benefit your guitar playing tremendously.

Chapter 7 Introduction To Basic Theory

Lesson 31: Understanding scales and keys

Understanding scales and keys is a vital part of music theory. It helps to navigate the fretboard, compose music, and improvise with confidence. Let's explore the basics to enhance your musical foundation.

The structure of scales:

Scales are a sequence of notes arranged in a certain order, serving as the building blocks of music.

Major scales: The major scale is characterized by its bright and happy sound. Each note numbered 1 - 8 corresponds to a degree of the scale. With the 8th note being the octave.

Minor scales: The minor scale conveys a more somber and emotional tone. There are several types of minor scales, including natural, melodic, and harmonic.

Each has a certain pattern of notes that contributes to its unique sound.

Understanding keys:

A key is defined by the scale it is based on, with one of its notes serving as the root. The key of C major uses the notes of the C major scale with the C being the root note.

Key signatures:

These represent whether a key has sharp or flat notes in it. They quickly allow a musician to identify the key to a piece of music.

Relative major & minor keys:

Each major key has a relative minor key that is made up of the same notes. Knowing this allows you to be more creative in your musicianship.

Applying scales and keys on the guitar:

Fretboard navigation:

Knowing scales helps you to move around the fretboard with ease. Practice playing scales in different positions and patterns to master them.

Improvising solos:

Scales provide a framework for improvisation. By understanding the key of a song, you can use the corresponding scale to create melodies and solos that fit.

Chord progressions:

Keys and scales are closely related to chord progressions. Get familiar with common chord progressions in various keys to improve your rhythm playing and songwriting.

Being proficient at playing rhythm is essential as an acoustic guitar player. Knowing about scales and keys and how they relate to each other, will help you to accomplish this.

With a little time given to it daily, it will eventually begin to make sense. But it must approached with discipline to get it right. It is one of the reasons most guitar players play by ear and bypass theory.

Remember, mastering keys and scales takes time and practice. Just like every other aspect of guitar playing. If you take it step-by-step and enjoy the process of discovering these musical elements, they can transform your playing.

Lesson 32: The root of chords in music

Understanding the root of chords is fundamental to understanding how music is structured. The root of a chord is the base note upon which the chord is built, and it identifies the chord's identity and tonal foundation.

Role in harmony:

The root note is often the lowest note you hear in the pitch of a chord. The foundation on which all other notes are based.

Triads:

These consist of three notes, the 1st, 3rd, and 5th of the scale they are derived from.

Chord extensions:

Beyond the root, you add notes called extensions. These include the other notes in the scale.

Understanding the root of the chord is essential to musicians and composers alike. It forms the basis for creating harmonies, developing chord progressions, and crafting music that resonates with listeners.

Lesson 33: How chords and scales relate

As we know from previous lessons, scales have a certain number of notes, and out of these scales, major & minor, we can create chords. Both major and minor. This is how chords and scales relate.

If you know the notes of any particular scale, and you know the note formula for any particular chord (triad = 1 3 5), you can create any chords you like out of that scale.

Musical alphabet: A A# B C C# D D# E F F# G G#

C major scale: C D E F G A B C

C major chord: 1 3 5 = C E G
C major sixth chord: 1 3 5 6 C E G A
C major seven chord: 1 3 5 7 = C E G B

Remember, scales provide the framework for which chords and progressions are built. Understanding their relationship allows for better improvisation, songwriting, and overall musicality.

As you continue to explore these concepts, you'll deepen your appreciation for how they contribute to the rich tapestry of music.

Lesson 34: Build confidence through understanding

Learning to play the acoustic guitar is more than just memorizing chords and practicing strumming patterns. It's about developing a deep understanding of the instrument.

It is through this understanding that build confidence in your playing. It not only enhances your technical skills but also allows you to express yourself musically and tackle new challenges with ease.

By understating such things as:

*<u>Choosing the right type of guitar.</u>

*<u>Mastering musical concepts.</u>

*<u>Developing technical skills.</u>

*<u>And expressing yourself.</u>

By building a strong foundation of understanding topics in these areas, you not only improve your technical abilities but also cultivate the confidence to explore new musical territories.

Lesson 35: Chapter 7 Quiz

Here you have learned about scales and keys, the root of guitar chords, how chords and scales relate, and how to build confidence through understanding these topics.

Q: How do scales and keys relate to music?
A: _____

Q: What is the purpose of the root of a guitar chord?
A: _____

Q: How do chords and scales relate to each other in music?
A: _____

Q: What three chords are presented in the C major scale?
A: _____

Q: What is building confidence through understanding about?
A: _____

Q: What four things are mentioned in chapter 34?
A: _____

There is no substitute for learning about these concepts to build confidence in your playing. Daily study and practice will do it.

Chapter 7 Summary

In this chapter, you have learned in the introduction to basic theory. This includes such things as understanding scales and keys, the root of chords in music, how scales and chords relate, and how to build confidence through understanding.

First, we look at scales and keys. This is helpful to know because scales allow you to know what key you are playing in, or what key a certain piece of music will be in.

Second, you learn that the root of a chord is the base note upon which all chords are built. It identifies the chord's character and helps with developing harmonies and chord progressions.

Third, how chords and scales relate. Scales provide the framework for which chords and progressions are built. This relationship allows for better improv and songwriting.

Lastly, learn to build confidence through better understanding. The more you know about these and other musical concepts, over time your confidence will grow and your musicianship will improve.

Chapter 8: Overcoming Challenges

Lesson 36: Common beginner mistakes

In this chapter, we are going to look at some common mistakes that beginning guitarists run into. This will give you insight on what to avoid or fix if you happen to run into any of them.

Improper hand positioning:

Beginners often struggle with proper hand positioning. Ensure that your hands are arched properly over the fretboard and you are pressing down with the tips of your fingers.

Neglecting the importance of rhythm:

Many players overlook and neglect the importance of creating and holding rhythm. Remember to work on this daily, and that using a metronome can help with this development.

Overlooking guitar tuning:

Playing guitar out of tune can be discouraging and hinder your progress. Make tuning your guitar a regular habit to ensure that you are always playing with the best sound possible.

Rushing through lessons:

It's common to rush through lessons with excitement, but don't do this. This will lead to poor technique and frustration later on. Take time to master each skill before moving to the next.

Inconsistent practice schedules:

Irregular practice habits can hinder progress. Establish a consistent practice schedule. Even if it's only 15 to 30 minutes a day, it will build muscle memory and skill set faster over time.

Avoiding challenging pieces:

Sticking only to what is easy for you will stunt growth. And this will hinder your playing in the long run. Gradually introduce more challenging pieces to push your boundaries.

Lack of patience and persistence:

Learning guitar is a gradual process that takes time. So develop patience and be persistent. As this will help you to get over hurdles and challenges.

By being aware of these common mistakes, you can proactively address them & ensure a more enjoyable learning experience.

Lesson 37: Tips for staying motivated

Learning to play the acoustic guitar is a rewarding journey, but like any skill it requires dedication and perseverance. Here are a few tips to help you stay motivated during the process.

Track your progress:

Noting what you've worked on and any improvements, will show how far you've come and keep you motivated to keep going.

Diversify your practice routine:

Incorporate different techniques, genres, and songs. This variety keeps the practice fun and interesting.

Stay consistent with practice.:

This will help you to develop the skill set needed to be a proficient acoustic guitar player. Don't overlook this.

By incorporating these few tips into your daily practice, you'll maintain your motivation and continue to have fun and enjoy an enriched experience learning to play the acoustic guitar.

Lesson 38: Setting music goals

Setting clear and achievable musical goals is a crucial step to ensure progress and stay motivated. Here are some strategies to help you set effective music goals.

Define your long-term vision:

Envision where you want to be in the long run. Your long-term vision will set as a guiding light, helping you stay focused daily.

Break it down into short-term goals:

Long-term visions are accomplished through smaller short-term goals. This makes it easier to achieve in the long run.

Be flexible and adaptable:

Be open to adjusting your goals to align with your growing skills and emerging musical interests. This keeps them relevant.

By setting clear and meaningful music goals, you'll create a structured path. This will guide your progress, embrace the process, and allow your passion, and musical voice to shine.

Lesson 39: Develop a practice routine

This is essential for progressing as an acoustic guitarist. It will help you achieve your music goals more effectively. Here are some key components to consider.

Focus on rhythm & timing:

Practice forming and transitioning between chords. Use a metronome to create rhythm and develop proper timing.

Incorporate basic theory:

Study different scales and keys to enhance the skill of forming chords. This will help improve and enhance your musicianship.

Study guitar notation:

This will allow you to learn songs quickly as well as improve your understanding of techniques and compositions.

By working on these concepts, you will develop a solid practice routine. Focus on them daily and you will be well on your way to becoming a highly skilled and expressive guitarist.

Lesson 40: Chapter 8 Quiz

Chapter 8 you learn some common mistakes that beginners make, tips for staying motivated, setting music goals, and how to develop a practice routine.

Q: What is the first lesson learned in chapter 8?
A: _____

Q: What do muting strings mean?
A: _____

Q: What do you accomplish by doing finger exercises?
A: _____

Q: What are some practice habits mentioned in this chapter?
A: _____

Q: What are these additional lessons so important?
A: _____

Q: Why is it important to have a goal and write it down?
A: _____

By doing the things stated in this chapter, you will be well ahead of the crowd. Most guitarists don't do these things.

Chapter 8 Summary

In this chapter, we have looked at some ways to overcome challenges. Common mistakes to avoid, tips for staying motivated, setting music goals, and developing a practice routine.

First, you want to make sure to focus on proper hand positioning. This will make a huge difference in forming chords, strumming and fingerpicking.

Two, we then discuss tips for staying motivated. This is one of the hardest things to accomplish when learning anything new. Use these to keep motivated with daily practice.

Third, you learn about setting music goals. These are designed to keep you on track and help you get to your result faster with less frustration.

Fourth, you learn about developing a solid practice routine. This can make a huge difference in the way your outcome is when playing the acoustic guitar.

It is highly recommended that you study this guide of best practices and use them to make your guitar playing more enjoyable, and your learning journey more educational.

92

Strumming To Success Conclusion

If you've made it this far I congratulate you on your accomplishments and say "Thank you for your purchase of this book and your time learning to play the guitar". You seem like the kind of student that I'd love to teach in person.

Learning the acoustic guitar opens up a world of musical possibilities and personal fulfillment. No matter if you are strumming chords or diving into the art of fingerpicking, each step forward will enrich your life.

The titles and structured guides provided in this training manual, cater to the fundamental principles needed to excel and enjoy the art of playing the acoustic guitar.

This variety of learning makes it possible for anyone to find a starting point that feels right. From understanding the anatomy of the acoustic guitar to mastering more advanced techniques. These resources underscore the importance of practice.

With consistent practice, patience, and passion, you can easily achieve your musical goals. That is, if you follow the guidelines to set your musical goals and use the tips suggested to help enhance your journey of accomplishing them.

Remember, music is a universal language, and the acoustic guitar is a timeless instrument that allows for rich expression and connection. As you continue on your musical journey, to make it fun, you must enjoy the process.

Celebrate musical victories, and don't get frustrated too much with challenges as they will pop up from time to time. This is all part of the learning curve. But most importantly, let your unique musical voice shine through.

If you find value in this book, please do let me know by leaving a review. Or, if you have any questions about any lessons in the book, be sure to let me know that as well. I will be happy to assist you.

Be sure to follow me on Instagram, like me on Facebook, and watch my free guitar lesson videos on YouTube.

Also, visit my website at DwaynesGuitarLessons.com.

Best of luck and have fun.

Sincerely, Dwayne Jenkins
Tritone Publishing. copyright © 2025

Other Books By Tritone Publishing

Learn To Play Rhythm Guitar

A comprehensive guide on the fundamental principles of playing rhythm guitar. Mainly for electric guitar, but many if not all the lessons can be utilized on the acoustic guitar as well.

Remember, rhythm guitar is vital to playing the guitar. No matter if it is played on acoustic or electric. So make sure to study this concept well and put it into practice daily.

Learn To Play The Ukulele

Learn To Play The Ukulele has been created specifically for students with no previous musical background. With lesson examples presented in today's most popular step-by-step format.

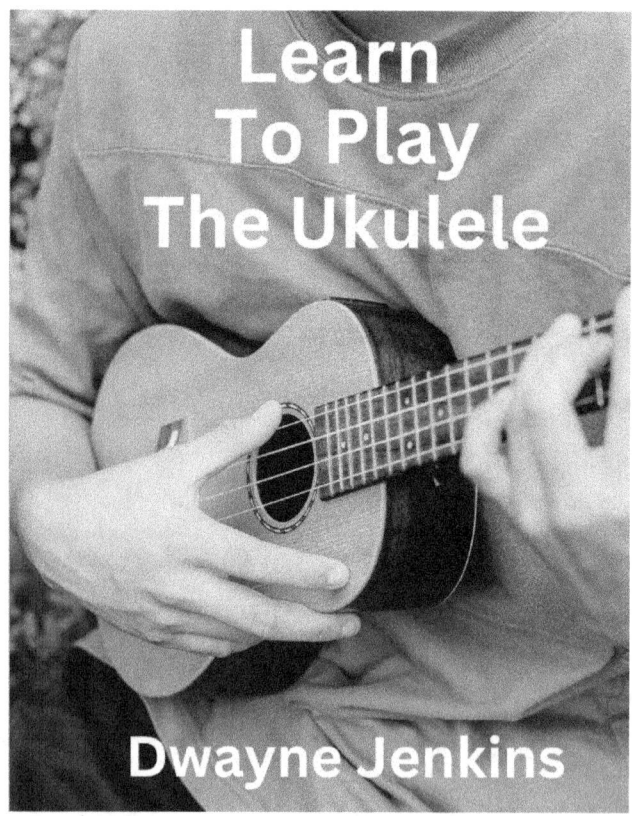

With everything needed to get started playing your favorite songs, this book will help you get started and keep you playing the instrument for years to come.

Learn Guitar Chord Theory:

Learn Guitar Chord Theory presents you with the fundamental principles needed to understand guitar chords. Not only how to form them, but why they are named as such. Like Gsus2, and E minor. You'll find out why in this book.

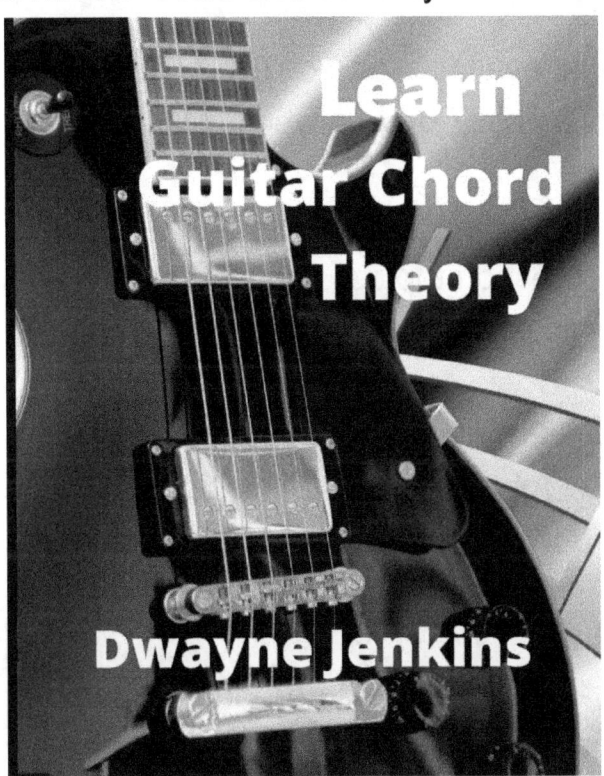

Along with that, you will learn how to recognize them when you see them in songbooks, as well as be able to use them in practical application.

All books are authored by Dwayne Jenkins, published by Tritone Publishing, and can be found worldwide.

They also can be found on Dwayne's website in digital format for quicker learning. Just download it onto your computer and start learning right away.

Guitar lesson videos are also available on YouTube. These are free and available 24 hours a day, 7 days a week, 365 days a year.

They cover a wide variety of lesson topics. Playing rhythm, lead, guitar maintenance, and product reviews.

Self-study is a great way to learn as it allows you to not only go at your own pace but also develop the skills of discipline and time management. These things can benefit you in other areas of your life as well.

If more help is needed, Dwayne also offers one-on-one private lessons. These are customized to fit the individual student's interests and skill level. Lessons can allow you to progress faster and have more fun in the process.

If you feel this option can help you, contact Dwayne today to set up a free consultation.

About the Author

Dwayne Jenkins is a professional guitar teacher, an accomplished musician, and an entrepreneur. He has been learning, playing, and teaching guitar lessons throughout Denver, CO for well over two decades.

He is now bringing his special training skills and methodology that have been honed and hand-crafted throughout the years on how to play to students around the world.

Dwayne has a unique exciting approach that gets students of all ages and skill levels enjoying the fun of playing guitar and ukulele. His enthusiasm and love for teaching shine through with every lesson that he creates.

His lessons are designed to enhance your ability to progress. No matter your reason for learning, there will always be something in Dwayne's books and products to help you achieve your dreams.

So if you're a student looking to start, or a student looking to further your education, be sure to get involved with Dwayne's guitar lessons and learn what so many people have already discovered why learning to play the guitar or ukulele, is one of the greatest things you can do for yourself

100

What Students Are Saying About Dwayne's Guitar Lessons

"Dwayne, thank you so much for everything you have taught me and done for me. You are an amazing guitarist and wonderful teacher" BJ.

"Dwayne, it has been a true pleasure to have you at our house each week! Ken & Trevor have learned so much through you and your teachings. Thank you!" Lisa

"Dwayne, thank you for being a great teacher and teaching me many great songs. This is a skill that will last me a lifetime." Danielle

"Dwayne, we want you to know we are honored to have you at the studio. We appreciate all that you do and are grateful that we can leave you in charge" Angie & Wilson M.E.C.

"Dwayne, we are so glad you are our Teacher. It's been three years already can you believe it? Thank you again. You're the best!" Chelsey & Lucas

"Dwayne, we are so glad that you are in our lives. Chelsey & Lucas enjoy their time with you and look up to you. Looking forward to another great year!" Love and best wishes, Ken & Sue.

"Dwayne, thank you so much for being not only an awesome guitar teacher, but an awesome friend as well" Kayla.

"Dwayne, thank you so much for all the years of doing lessons. You have been very patient with my progress helped me to build confidence in myself and inspired me to follow my dreams. And in doing so you have become a great friend" Jake.

"Dwayne, thank you for teaching Nick guitar so well. He loves it and is getting quite good fast. I'm amazed!" Jane.

"Dwayne, Thank you so much for teaching me every Saturday and not only teaching me guitar but also about life and helping me with setting my goals. You are a great teacher, mentor, and the best friend ever" Carson.

"There is not another person I would want to be teaching me a guitar! His 1 on 1 teaching makes learning guitar very personal & exhilarating. He teaches at your pace and takes pride in what YOU want to learn. The best part…if Dwayne doesn't know a song a student wants to play, he takes time out of the week to learn it His teaching comes to life in my performance and has progressed over the last 8 years. Words cannot describe how amazing a teacher, rockstar, and true friend Dwayne has become to me" Dominic.

Appendix 1: Chord reference guide

Once you learn to read chord charts, you can play an unlimited amount of them. Here is a chord chart reference guide that can be used to increase your guitar chord vocabulary.

Major chords:

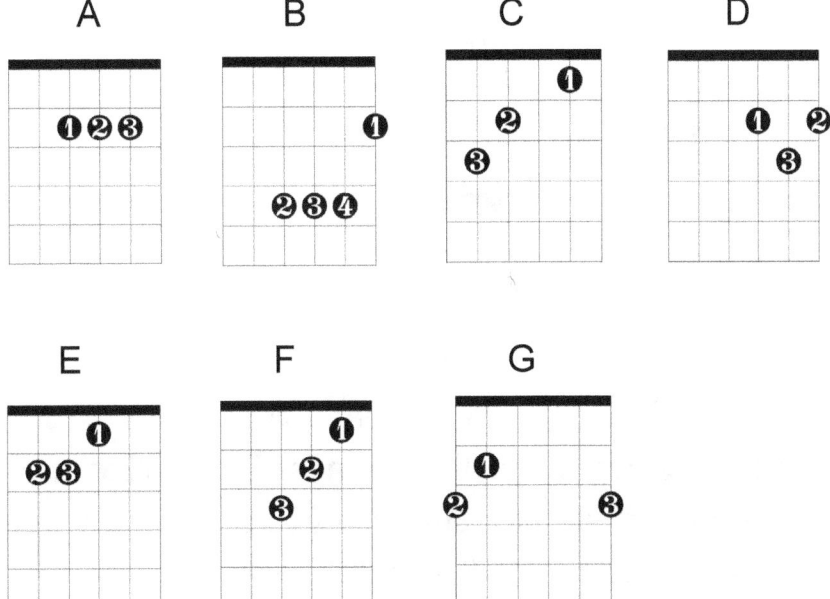

Some of these you already know. They are presented here again as a reference. Focus on the new chords you don't know and add them to your chord progressions.

Minor chords:

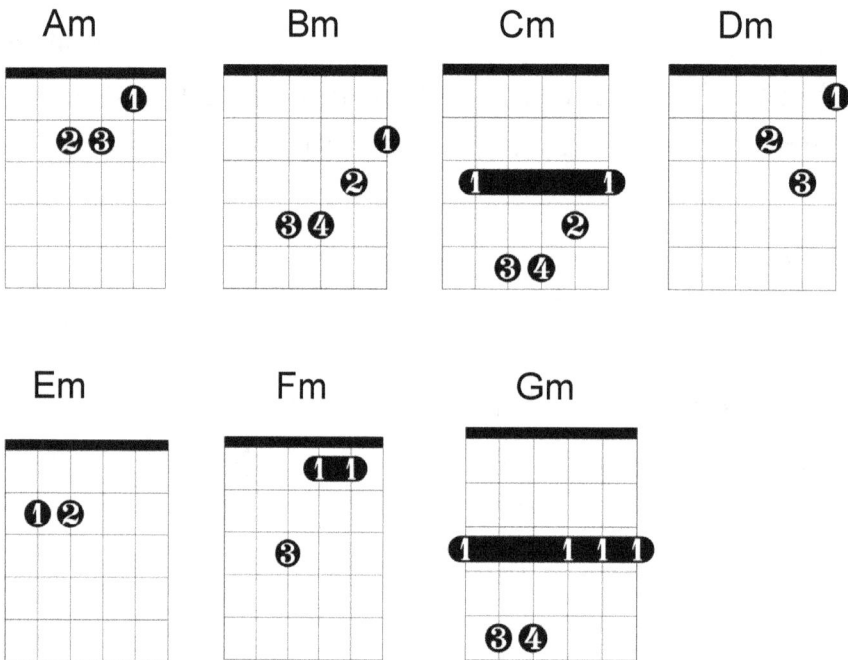

When it comes to the C and G minor chords, you will need to barre your index finger across multiple strings. This will take a bit of getting your fingers used to, but once you do, you'll be able to play chords further up the fretboard.

When you form chords like these, they are called barre chords, and they are very useful in playing acoustic guitar.

Seventh chords:

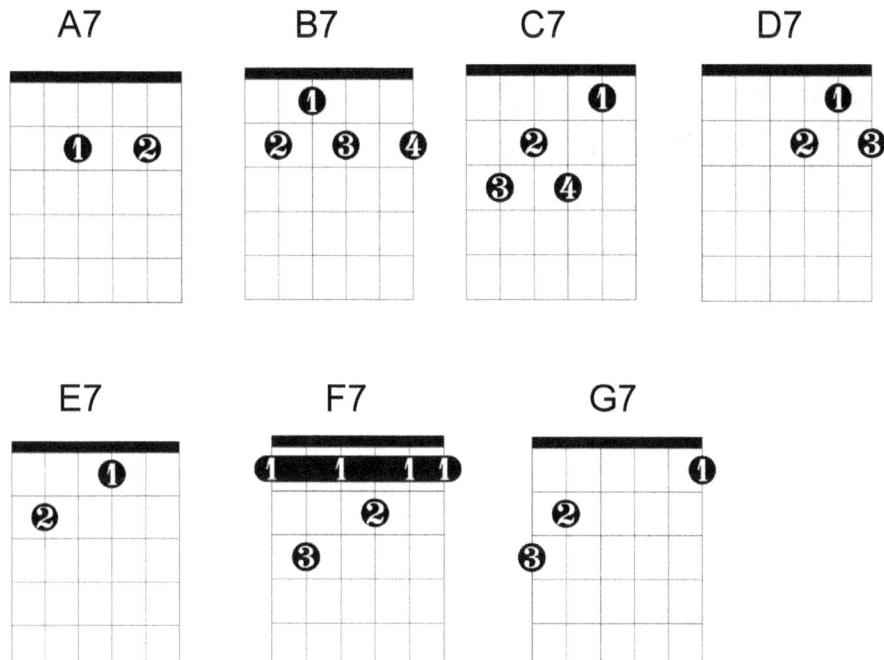

Seventh chords are another popular chord type that are very common in songs. Be sure to learn these and add them to your chord collection.

There are a lot more chords to learn. These are just some of the most common ones. Their purpose is to help you establish how to recognize them and play ones that you don't already know.

Appendix 2: Scale reference guide

Scales are the foundation of chords.

Chromatic scale:
A A# B C C# D D# E F F# G G#

C major scale: = no sharps
C D E F G A B C

G major scale: = 1 sharp
G A B C D E F# G

D major scale: = 2 sharps
D E F# G A B C# D

A major scale: = 3 sharps
A B C# D E F# G# A

E major scale: = 4 sharps
E F# G# A B C# D# E

B major scale: = 5 sharps
B C# D# E F# G# A# B

F major scale: = 1 flat
F G A Bb C D E F

Relative minor scales:

A minor scale: same notes as C major
A B C D E F G A

E minor scale: same notes as G major
E F# G A B C D E

B minor scale: same notes as D major
B C# D E F# G A B

F sharp minor scale: same notes as A major
F# G# A B C# D E F#

C sharp minor: same notes as E major
C# D# E F# G# A B C#

G sharp minor scale: same notes as B major
G# A B C# D# E F# G#

D minor scale: same notes as F major
D E F G A Bb C D

Knowing the relative minor scale is great because it allows you to switch between the two relatively easily. Study these and remember which minor scale goes with which major scale.

Scales theory continued:

As I stated before, knowing the notes of any scale can help you out when it comes to writing compositions, creating chord progressions, and creating melody lines and guitar solos.

Knowing what keys share the same notes allows you to create a more diverse shift in tone when it comes to chords and melodies. Going from C major to A minor, or from G major, to E minor is a great way to start a chord progression.

Playing a guitar solo in the key of A minor and then switching to a scale in C major will work because the two scales have the same notes. By doing this you can add a variation in color, emotion, and texture to your music.

This knowledge can also simplify your understanding of key changes, and chord progressions that move back and forth between major chords and the relative minor. By doing this, the composition can create different emotions such as tension, and relaxation, or light and shadow.

You don't need to know massive music theory, but I recommend you learn the basics of it. It will help fill in some of the gaps when questions arise on your journey to learning to play the greatest instrument in the world, the acoustic guitar.

Taking Private Lessons

If you'd like more of a personalized experience, it can be highly beneficial to take private lessons. This option can be very enlightening as it allows the instruction to be tailored to your skill level and interests.

If you have specific musical goals, taking private lessons can help you get there faster. Provided, that you find the right instructor.

With the right guitar teacher, you can learn techniques that cater specifically to your goals and can be taught in-depth how to avoid bad habits and get immediate feedback on how you are progressing.

You also can get the teacher's own experience on certain techniques and topics that will help you to avoid mistakes and develop techniques and understanding faster than you normally would.

Overall, private guitar lessons can be a great way to navigate the mystery of music, as it provides a custom learning experience. Which allows you to progress at your own pace and learn what is of interest to you.

www.ingramcontent.com/pod-product-compliance
Lightning Source LLC
Chambersburg PA
CBHW082210070526
44585CB00020B/2360